SPEAK Life

Healing the Hurt of Verbal Abuse

Copyright ©2024 Antonia Agbonkpolor
All rights reserved.
ISBN 978-1-913455-67-5
No part of this book shall be reproduced or transmitted in any form or by any means, electronic or mechanical, including photocopying, recording, or by any information retrieval system without prior written permission of the author and publisher.
Published by Scribblecity Publications United Kingdom.
Printed in Great Britain.
Although every precaution has been taken in the preparation of this book, the publisher and author assume no responsibility for errors or omissions. Neither is any liability assumed for damages resulting from the use of this information contained herein.
Scriptures taken from the Holy Bible, New International Version®, NIV®. Copyright © 1973, 1978, 1984, 2011 by Biblica, Inc.™ Used by permission of Zondervan. All rights reserved worldwide. www.zondervan.com The "NIV" and "New International Version" are trademarks registered in the United States Patent and Trademark Office by Biblica, Inc.™

Scripture quotations are from The ESV® Bible (The Holy Bible, English Standard Version®), © 2001 by Crossway, a publishing ministry of Good News Publishers. Used by permission. All rights reserved

Scripture quotations marked (NLT) are taken from the Holy Bible, New Living Translation, copyright © 1996, 2004, 2015 by Tyndale House Foundation. Used by permission of Tyndale House Publishers, Inc., Carol Stream, Illinois 60188. All rights reserved.

Scripture taken from the New King James Version®. Copyright © 1982 by Thomas Nelson. Used by permission. All rights reserved.

Dedication

*To God Almighty, whose wisdom and guidance have
enabled me to bring this book to life.
Your grace has been my steadfast foundation.*

And to the individuals whose stories are the heart of these pages.

Thank you for sharing.

Acknowledgements

Firstly, I thank God Almighty for my life and for positioning me for this opportunity.

Secondly, to my Pastors, Pastor Clem and Apostle Marjorie Esomowei, for their support with this book, along with their prayers and teachings.

I would like to express my heartfelt gratitude to my parents, Lawrence Oladokun and Josephine Oladokun, for bringing me into this world and for their unwavering love and prayers.

Special thanks to my friends who have generously shared their stories, enriching the content of this book.

I am very grateful to my husband, John, and my children, Michael and Daniel Agbonkpolor, for their unwavering support and for being my biggest supporters. I am truly blessed to have you guys.

I also extend my appreciation to my publishers for their assistance and guidance throughout the publishing process.

Finally, to the readers, thank you for embracing this book. I hope its contents provide comfort, empowerment, and guidance to all those affected by verbal abuse.

Thank you.
Antonia Agbonkpolor

Foreword

Thank you Antonia for making out the time to write this book. Reading through it, I could feel the passion of a woman who wants to see healing come to as many people as possible from the pain of their past, from words released on them by strangers and loved ones.

In this book *Speak Life*, Antonia presents a strong case for speaking words that heal, over ourselves, our family and our spouses. We are able to look beyond the spiritual impact of negative words. The book is for anyone who wants to have a balanced perspective of the impact of negative words as Antonia helps us to delve into the spiritual, psychological, sociological and biological implications of careless and carefree words.

Antonia exposes dark and vile issues around verbal abuse and the lasting and inexpugnable scars these words can leave on a person, old or young.

It's great to see amongst other solutions, that we are presented with strong prayers to support people who have been maimed through negative words

This book *Speak Life* by Antonia Agbonkpolor comes highly recommended for positive parenting and for those aspiring to meet their couple goals. When you get a copy, you are encouraged to also get a copy/copies for a friend, parents and newly weds.

Apostle Marjorie Esomowei
Pastor, Coach, Life Strategist

Contents

Foreword	xi
Introduction	15
Chapter 1 **The Power of Spoken Word**	19
Chapter 2 *Verbal Abuse in Childhood:* **The Seed of Negative Words**	22
Chapter 3 *Verbal Abuse in Childhood:* **Positive Communication**	35
Chapter 4 *Spousal Relationships:* **The Poisonous Power of Words**	44
Chapter 5 **Scars of Verbal Abuse**	49
Chapter 6 **How to Receive Healing**	53
Chapter 7 **Forgiveness**	64
Chapter 8 **Replacing Fear with Faith**	68

Chapter 9
**Spotting Verbal Abuse
in Schools and Workplaces**   72

Chapter 10
Moving Forward   75

Chapter 11
Making a Change   78

Chapter 12
Prayer Points   82

INTRODUCTION

The inspiration for this book goes beyond personal experiences, it stems from a calling to shed light on a pervasive issue that affects countless individuals across cultural and generational divides. Through numerous encounters with friends, colleagues, and acquaintances seeking solace and prayer amidst the impact of verbal abuse, I have witnessed the urgent need for compassionate intervention.

Verbal abuse leaves deep emotional scars that can hinder personal growth and erode self-esteem. It is my conviction that faith, rooted in the healing power of God's love, offers a transformative path towards restoration and empowerment.

INTRODUCTION

Yet, even in our darkest moments, we are reminded that we are never truly alone. As written in Psalm 34:18, "The Lord is close to the broken hearted and saves those who are crushed in spirit." In the depths of our despair, God's comforting presence surrounds us, offering solace and strength to those who call upon His name.

Verbal abuse can sneak into every corner of our lives, disrupting the love and trust we hold dear. When parents say unkind things, or partners throw hurtful words, or even when caregivers put us down, It's like the words leave a stain on our hearts that's hard to scrub off.

However, as cherished children of God, we ought to remember our inherent worth and dignity. Genesis 1:27 affirms, "So God created mankind in his own image, in the image of God he created them; male and female he created them." No words spoken against us should diminish the beauty and value that God has bestowed upon each of us.

This book delves in on the painful topic of verbal abuse, the ways it affects us, and how faith can help us heal. So, let's journey together, find our strength, and rewrite our stories with courage and faith.

The Bible offers profound wisdom on the power of words and the importance of healing from wounds inflicted by them. **Proverbs 18:21** reminds us that "Death and life are in the power of the tongue, and those who love it will eat its fruits." Our words have the capacity to bring **life** or **death**, to **build up** or **tear down**.

Recognising this truth underscores the significance of addressing verbal abuse and embracing healing through positive, life-giving Bible based communication. Scripture affirms the transformative power of faith in overcoming adversity and finding healing. In **Isaiah 53:5**, we read, "But he was pierced for our transgressions; he was crushed for our iniquities; upon him was the chastisement that brought us peace, and with his wounds we are healed." This profound verse speaks of Christ's sacrifice, which not only offers spiritual healing but also extends to emotional and psychological restoration from all forms of abuse, including verbal.

Throughout this book, we will draw inspiration from biblical narratives of resilience and redemption, exploring how individuals like Joseph, Job, and David navigated through deep wounds inflicted by words. Their stories

INTRODUCTION

serve as beacons of hope, demonstrating that healing and restoration are possible even in the face of profound pain and suffering. Let us embark on this journey of healing together, guided by faith and anchored in the promise of God's transformative love.

Chapter 1

THE POWER OF SPOKEN WORD

Verbal Abuse

As mentioned in the introduction, the motivation behind writing this book is deeply personal and originates from a burden that has weighed heavily on my heart through countless encounters with individuals seeking solace and prayer amidst the impact of verbal abuse.

It's important to note in our relationships with others, words are like powerful tools that can either build people up or tear them down. "Death and life are in the power of the tongue, and those who love it will eat its fruits." **Proverbs 18:21.** Verbal abuse happens when words are used to hurt someone emotionally. The devastating effects are evident across diverse cultures and communities. Numerous lives have been marred by the cruel words and actions of some family members, caregivers, and spouses, and their stories paint a stark picture of the lasting and damaging effects of verbal abuse in one form or another. On self-esteem, relationships, and overall well-being.

When verbal abuse occurs in childhood, if not resolved may reverberate into adulthood, displaying such tendencies in parenting, marriage and society. Like the maxim, 'Hurt people, hurt people'. It can easily become cyclical. In other cases, it can cause paralysis to the child's self-esteem in their later life with the person carrying the perception of not being "good enough", feeling they are a failure.

The Word of God is God's medicine for bringing healing, restoring dignity and emotional well-being. The bible says Jesus came to set the captives free in **Isaiah 61:1,**
> "The Spirit of the Lord GOD is upon Me, Because the LORD has anointed Me To preach good tidings to the poor; He has sent Me to heal the broken-hearted, To proclaim liberty to the captives, And the opening of the prison to those who are bound;"

This same scripture was quoted by Jesus himself at the beginning of his ministry in Luke 4:17-20.

My prayer is that this book becomes a source of hope and healing for anyone who's been hurt by words, and like in **Isaiah 61:1**, They can break free from the pain of verbal abuse and realise just how valuable they are in God's eyes.

Although verbal abuse can cast a dark shadow, through faith there is power and healing in the word of God.
Romans 8:1 clearly states, "There is therefore now no condemnation to those who are in Christ Jesus, who do not walk according to the flesh, but according to the Spirit."

Together, let's take this journey toward reclaiming our voices and rewriting our stories with courage and confidence as God has intended.

What is Verbal Abuse?

Verbal abuse is when someone says unkind things to you in either a passive or aggressive tone, even though they don't physically hurt you. It's insults, name-calling, or constantly pointing out your mistakes. Even making you doubt yourself or scaring you with threats can be a form of verbal abuse.

Chapter 2

VERBAL ABUSE IN CHILDHOOD:
THE SEED OF NEGATIVE WORDS

This book sheds light on a critical issue that affects individuals worldwide, stemming from generational patterns and misunderstandings about human nature. For a long time I believed that my challenges were just as a result of the verbal abuse I experienced from people in my life. but now I know that although Adam and Eve had the best parent - God, they were deceived by the serpent who lied to them about their identity. Their acceptance of these words ultimately brought death and destruction to all creation. This is to say that negative words can come from people or within us. There is an inner voice of the enemy that speaks constantly to us that we are worthless in spite of all the positive affirmations from people around us.

Like many others, my friends and colleagues in their upbringing experienced verbal abuse as a form of discipline. Influenced by their own upbringing, their families believed that tough words were necessary for character development. They thought they were being firm and teaching important lessons, but they were unaware of the harmful impact of negative words on children. Most people do not know that whenever you open your mouth, you can either be Satan's advocate or God's mouthpiece speaking life or death.

Most parents genuinely love their children and want the best for them. Unfortunately, due to their own upbringing, they may have adopted negative words, thinking it would toughen their children for success. However, some parents eventually embraced the teachings of the Scriptures and repented of using negative words. They turned to prayer for their children's well-being. And as the children grow up into adulthood, they recall the ache of hearing hurtful words directed at them as children. Each word felt like a weight on their shoulders, shaping their beliefs about themselves and their capabilities. It may take years of discovering your identity in Christ and prayers to untangle the web of negativity woven by those early experiences.

In exploring their experiences, we uncover a generational pattern shaped by their families' influences. This cycle of verbal abuse, rooted in misunderstanding and cultural norms, underscores the importance of addressing these harmful behaviours and seeking healing through faith and positive communication. Through their journeys, we glimpse the transformative power of embracing God's love and breaking free from the cycle of verbal abuse.

Through heartfelt conversations with friends, colleagues, and family, I discovered that verbal abuse is more common than people realise and transcends cultural boundaries. Some individuals seem resilient to its effects, while others, like me were sensitive and, as a result, internalised every hurtful word, which subsequently impacted my self esteem and emotional well-being.

One friend shared how she struggled for years to overcome the hurtful words spoken by her father. Another recounted constant criticism from her mother, which affected her confidence well into adulthood. These stories highlight the pervasive nature of verbal abuse and its lasting impact on personal growth. I wish they could have saved themselves years of pain by keying in to the Word of God and using it to negate verbal abuse. **Isaiah 54:17,** "No weapon formed against you shall prosper and every tongue that rises against you in judgement, you shall prove to be in the wrong."

Nowadays, you would think that most parents get, that words have serious power, they can either build you up or tear you down. We have multitudes of self-help motivational gurus who preach about positive thinking and words. Yet, with all this understanding, it's heartbreaking to still hear about kids getting hurt by negative words. It's like, we know better, so why isn't it changing? It is clear to me that the world is trying to solve a spiritual problem while ignoring the transforming power of God's word.

Stated in **Ephesians 4:29,** "Let no corrupting talk come out of your mouths, but only such as is good for building up, as fits the occasion, that it may give grace to those who hear." This verse emphasises the importance of speaking words that build others up and impart grace, reflecting the transformative impact of positive communication.

A lady who endured relentless verbal abuse from her parents throughout her upbringing was repeatedly called "stupid" and "crazy". Her aspirations and talents were dismissed and despite excelling academically, she struggled with deep-seated insecurities, believing she would never amount to anything.

After experiencing such verbal attack, and if we don't use the word of God to neutralise it, individuals often find themselves on distinct paths.

Individuals who have experienced verbal abuse handle its effects in various ways, and can be categorised into different responses: "**The Replicator,**" "**The Survivor,**" or "**The Victor.**"

> 1. **The Replicator**: This represents someone who unwittingly replicates the harmful attitudes and behaviour of the abuser, perpetuating negative patterns in their own life.
>
> 2. **The Survivor**: This signifies someone who has been deeply impacted by verbal abuse, often making valid excuses for their struggles, and feeling trapped by their past experiences.

3. **The Victor:** This denotes someone who rises above their past trauma and works diligently towards personal growth and success, refusing to let their history define their full potential. To be truly a victor, you would have to completely depend on the grace found in the Word of God because it is the only thing that will keep you from harbouring any inner hurt or pain.

In conversations with friends who faced verbal abuse in childhood, I've observed diverse reactions. Some friends were deeply affected, finding the words hurtful and damaging, while others appeared unaffected outwardly, though they acknowledge some underlying hurt.

Reflecting on these discussions, I didn't encounter anyone who viewed verbal abuse as beneficial. Each person acknowledged a degree of hurt, even if they seemed resilient outwardly. For instance, a friend shared about being verbally abused by his father. Initially, he seemed unaffected by the words, displaying characteristics of "The Victor." However, upon deeper reflection, he admitted harbouring resentment and hatred toward his father for a long time. Despite appearing resilient, there was still underlying hurt and a journey toward forgiveness which can only be achieved through the power of the Holy Spirit. **Luke 4:18**, "The Spirit of the Lord is upon me, because he hath anointed me to preach the gospel to the poor; he hath sent me to heal the broken-hearted, to preach deliverance to the captives, and recovering of sight to the blind, to set at liberty them that are bruised."

These experiences remind me of biblical stories that illustrate the complexity of human emotions and responses to adversity. In Genesis, we see Joseph's story, where he faced betrayal and mistreatment by his own brothers. Despite enduring hardship, Joseph emerged as a victor, ultimately forgiving his brothers and embracing God's purpose for his life (Genesis 37-50). Joseph's resilience and capacity for forgiveness exemplify the transformative power of faith in overcoming adversity.

Similarly, King David's life offers insights into the complexities of emotional healing. After David's grievous sin with Bathsheba, he experienced the discipline of God but eventually found restoration and forgiveness through repentance (Psalm 51). David's journey highlights the importance of acknowledging pain and seeking reconciliation with God and others.

Scripture also reminds us of the significance of forgiveness in healing from emotional wounds.

In **Matthew 6:14-15,** Jesus teaches, "For if you forgive others their trespasses, your heavenly Father will also forgive you, but if you do not forgive others their trespasses, neither will your Father forgive your trespasses." This verse underscores the transformative power of forgiveness in releasing the burden of hurt and embracing healing.

In summary, individuals affected by verbal abuse navigate their healing journey in unique ways, embodying characteristics of "The Replicator," "The Survivor," or "The Victor." Through biblical examples and teachings, we learn valuable lessons about resilience, forgiveness, and the transformative power of faith in overcoming the lasting effects of verbal abuse.

Each person's healing path is unique and requires patience and understanding the ability of the Word of God to heal us completely. Some may feel empowered by their experiences, while others may need time to navigate their emotions and rebuild their confidence.

Healing from verbal abuse may not be linear, for some it may be a journey marked by ups and downs, setbacks and triumphs. It's about reclaiming one's voice, rewriting one's narrative, and forging a path towards a brighter, empowered future.

Effects of Verbal Abuse on Children

Children can be really hurt by this, especially when it comes from their own parents. Sometimes, parents think being tough and using harsh words will make their kids behave better or stronger. But it actually makes them feel really bad about themselves.

It's unfair when parents play favourites either, like when the sister gets all the praise and gifts, and the other gets yelled at or ignored. That can really mess with the head, and it's just not right.

I remember my cousin going through something similar in his family. His dad used to say unkind things to him because his sister did better in school. He never got any praise or presents, just harsh words which made him feel really small and worthless.

The Bible talks about how powerful our words are and how important it is to use them wisely.

In **Proverbs 18:21**, it says, "The tongue has the power of life and death, and those who love it will eat its fruit." This means our words can either lift someone up or tear them down, especially in families. So, it's important to be kind and loving with what we say, especially to our children.

The other day, I was speaking with a close friend, who shared that she had a habit of shouting at her children when she is angry, often saying things like, "Are you mad?" or "Are you crazy?" As a parent myself, with two boys, I understand the challenges of parenting and the importance of discipline.

In biblical context, the "rod" symbolises guidance and correction, rather than mere physical punishment. It serves as a metaphor for loving discipline aimed at shaping character and behaviour, reflecting God's correction of those He loves, as stated in **Hebrews 12:6 (AMP)**: "For the Lord disciplines and corrects those whom He loves, And He punishes every son whom He receives and welcomes [to His heart]." Parents are called to correct their children with love and wisdom, ensuring that discipline serves a constructive purpose.

Proverbs 13:24 (NIV) affirms this principle: "Whoever spares the rod hates their children, but the one who loves their children is careful to discipline them." This verse underscores the importance of disciplined guidance in fostering a child's growth and understanding of right and wrong.

I believe that discipline can include punishment to enforce boundaries, but the key lies in ensuring the child understands why they are being corrected. For instance, a light tap with a ruler on the knuckles can be used to capture a child's attention and communicate that their current behaviour is unacceptable. However, it is equally important to explain to the child the reasons behind the punishment. In many abusive situations, children endure harsh physical punishment without understanding the purpose or learning from the experience.

King David faced consequences for his actions (2 Samuel 12) but experienced God's forgiveness and restoration through repentance.

As parents, we are called to emulate God's loving discipline with our children. Correction should be firm yet compassionate, aimed at nurturing character and instilling values. **Proverbs 22:6 (NKJV):** "Train up a child in the way he should go, And when he is old he will not depart from it." It's about guiding our children toward maturity and responsibility, just as God guides us in our spiritual journey. Let us correct with love and grace, following the example of our Heavenly Father.

There was a man whose rediscovery of faith played a pivotal role in his healing from verbal abuse. Through spiritual guidance, and renewing his mind through word of God, he learned to let go of limiting beliefs and embrace his true worth as a child of God. He discovered that it was only through the word of God that the whispering negative thoughts of unworthiness and condemnation sown through verbal abuse could be defeated. As written in **Isaiah 54:17,** "No weapon formed against you shall prosper, **And every tongue which rises against you in judgement You shall condemn.**" Says the LORD. He was also reminded of God's promise in **Jeremiah 29:11,** "For I know the thoughts that I think toward you, says the LORD, thoughts of peace and not of evil, to give you a future and a hope."

The man's faith journey illustrates the transformative power of spiritual healing through the Word of God. This newfound confidence empowered Him to pursue his goals and cultivate healthy relationships.

Chapter 3

Verbal Abuse in Childhood:
POSITIVE COMMUNICATION

Using intentional and positive language is crucial for parents in nurturing their children's emotional well-being and building strong bonds. It's not just about what you say but how you say it.

When parents communicate with their children in a respectful and affirming manner, it creates a sense of trust and mutual respect.

Positive communication isn't just about the words we use; it's about creating an atmosphere of understanding and support. By engaging in meaningful conversations and truly listening to their children, parents can show that they value their thoughts and feelings. After all, just like adults, children are still learning and growing every day, and they rely on their parents to guide them through life's ups and downs.

Proverbs 16:24 (ESV): "Gracious words are like a honeycomb, sweetness to the soul and health to the body." **Proverbs 15:4** says, "A gentle tongue is a tree of life; But perverseness therein is a breaking of the spirit."

These scriptures highlight the profound impact of gracious words on our emotional and physical health, emphasising the importance of positive communication.

Effective parenting involves building healthy relationships through communication. By listening actively and responding with empathy, parents cultivate a supportive environment where children feel safe expressing themselves.

Correcting a child and explaining why, in my experience, works best rather than resorting to severe punishment or hurtful words. **Proverbs 23:13-14:** [13] "Do not withhold discipline from a child; although you strike him with a rod, he will not die. ¹⁴ Strike him with a rod, and you will deliver his soul from Sheol."

Proverbs 23:13(MSG): "Don't be afraid to correct your young ones; a spanking won't kill them. A good spanking, in fact, might save them from something worse than death." A lady experienced a significant transformation in her relationship with her son through the power of positive communication. Previously, she would often react with anger and punishment when her son misbehaved, resulting in strained interactions and misunderstandings.

Recognising the need for change, she embarked on a journey of positive parenting. Instead of reacting impulsively, she began actively listening to her son's concerns and explaining expectations calmly and patiently. This shift in approach created a supportive environment where her son felt valued and understood. Disciplining angrily is dangerous and does not produce a harvest of righteousness this is according to **James 1:20**, "For the anger of man does not produce the righteousness of God."

Over time, her efforts bore fruit as their bond grew stronger and her son started taking responsibility for his actions. By consistently using positive communication techniques, she nurtured mutual respect and trust within their relationship, fostering a positive and harmonious family dynamic.

This lady's story serves as a powerful reminder of the transformative impact of intentional and empathetic communication in parenting. Through her commitment to positive communication, She not only strengthened her relationship with her son but also empowered him to develop essential life skills and emotional resilience.

Similarly, just as in the case of those mentioned in the examples, I have found that positive communication with my children has led to them trusting me and confiding in me about most things. By fostering this trust through positive communication, my children feel comfortable discussing their thoughts and experiences with me rather than seeking advice from strangers.

Parents can implement practical tools and strategies to enhance positive communication by:

- Paying full attention to children's thoughts and feelings without interruptions. By encouraging them to allow their thoughts and feelings to be shaped by the word of God, will help foster healthy family relationships. **Romans 8:14** states, "For as many as are led by the Spirit of God, they are the sons of God."

- Using words of affirmation and encouragement to build confidence and resilience.

- Communicating expectations calmly and respectfully to foster mutual understanding.

Colossians 4:6 (ESV) reminds us, "Let your speech always be gracious, seasoned with salt, so that you may know how you ought to answer each person." This verse encourages us to speak with grace and wisdom, considering the impact of our words on others.

It's important to know navigating challenges in communication requires patience and perseverance. By addressing conflicts calmly and seeking mutual understanding, one can resolve misunderstandings and strengthen their relationships.

Over time, I have realised the importance of fostering

positive communication and mutual respect especially within the parent-child relationship. By embracing empathy and understanding, parents create a supportive environment where children not only feel safe but also thrive emotionally and socially.

Through deliberate communication and positive reinforcement by speaking the word of God over their kids, parents empower their children to express themselves freely and navigate challenges with confidence. This approach builds trust and strengthens family bonds, laying a foundation for a strong spiritual life which leads to healthy relationships and emotional well-being.

In summarising this chapter, the journey from fear to understanding has reinforced the transformative power of Bible based positive parenting. By prioritising love, empathy, and respectful communication, parents can create an environment where children feel valued and respected. Together, let us embrace positive parenting practices that promote emotional growth, strengthen family dynamics, and nurture the next generation of confident and resilient individuals.

Positive parenting begins with establishing a foundation of trust and mutual respect. It involves prioritising open communication and active listening to create a supportive environment where children feel valued and understood.

A mother of two, previously had a habit of yelling at her kids when she was angry with them. I noticed this behaviour and, drawing from my own experiences, I gently confronted her about it. We had several discussions where I emphasised that her children were more likely to respond positively and confide in her if she communicated calmly instead of raising her voice. As a joke, I also mentioned that it would be beneficial for her blood pressure to reduce yelling, which is also true.

Before our conversations, her household often echoed with raised voices during moments of frustration. This communication style strained their relationships and left her children feeling misunderstood and anxious.

As shown in **Proverbs 15:1 (NIV),** A gentle answer turns away wrath, but a harsh word stirs up anger." The scripture underscores the importance of responding with gentleness and empathy in our interactions with our children.

So, through our discussions and her own reflection, she began implementing positive communication techniques. Instead of yelling, she started listening actively and validating her children's feelings. Over time, her household became calmer and more harmonious.

Her efforts paid off as her children began to open up more and seek her guidance during challenging times. They felt respected and understood, which strengthened their bond with their mother.

Positive parenting encourages a growth mindset by emphasising effort and resilience over perfection. By praising perseverance and celebrating progress, parents instil confidence and motivation in their children.

Encouraging open and honest communication within the family can strengthen bonds and create a supportive environment where conflicts are resolved peacefully. Teaching problem-solving skills and emphasising the importance of compromise empowers family members to work together towards common goals, fostering unity and understanding. This approach promotes healthy relationships and cultivates a sense of belonging and mutual respect within the family.

The bible states in, **Ephesians 4:2 (NIV)**, Be completely humble and gentle; be patient, bearing with one another in love." This scripture emphasises the virtues of humility, patience, and love in maintaining healthy relationships within the family.

In summary, positive communication and loving discipline which hurts is the cornerstone of effective parenting. By adopting empathetic and affirming language, parents foster trust, nurture emotional intelligence, and strengthen family bonds. As we continue to embrace positive parenting practices guided by biblical principles, we create a nurturing environment where our children can thrive and grow into confident individuals.

Chapter 4

SPOUSAL RELATIONSHIPS:
THE POISONOUS POWER OF WORDS

Unfortunately, many married people are blinded by their emotional attachment in marriage and do not realise that their spouses are actually being used by the enemy to attack them. You must treat verbal abuse in marriage as you would in other situations by seeing Satan as your enemy not your spouse.

Words spoken in marriage hold tremendous weight, capable of either strengthening the bond between partners or creating toxicity and distance. Verbal attacks, criticism, and contempt can erode trust, respect, and emotional intimacy.

Scripture: **Proverbs 12:18**: "The words of the reckless pierce like swords, but the tongue of the wise brings healing."

In **Ephesians 4:29 (NIV)**, we are reminded of the power of words: "Do not let any unwholesome talk come out of your mouths, but only what is helpful for building others up according to their needs, that it may benefit those who listen."

Effective communication is the lifeblood of a healthy marriage. However, hurtful language, manipulation, and belittling words can lead to frequent misunderstandings and conflicts, ultimately causing emotional disconnection and alienation. **Proverbs 15:1** reminds us, "A soft answer turns away wrath, But a harsh word stirs up anger." How we communicate is important in fostering a healthy relationship.

Scripture: **Ephesians 4:29**: "Do not let any unwholesome talk come out of your mouths, but only what is helpful for building others up according to their needs, that it may benefit those who listen."

In many cases, a spouse who uses verbal poison may be replicating learned behaviour from their upbringing.

Growing up in an environment where verbal abuse was normalised, they may unknowingly perpetuate this destructive pattern in their own marriage. Recognising this root cause is crucial for initiating healing and transformation.

Scripture: **Matthew 15:18:** "But the things that come out of a person's mouth come from the heart, and these defile them."

Verbal poison impedes emotional intimacy and vulnerability between spouses. When one partner feels consistently attacked or devalued through words, they may withdraw emotionally to protect themselves from further hurt, hindering the deep connection necessary for a healthy marital bond.

Scripture: **Colossians 3:19**: "Husbands, love your wives and do not be harsh with them."

Recognising the impact of verbal poison is the first step toward healing and restoring spousal relationships. Couples can embark on a journey of reconciliation by fostering open, respectful communication and replacing hurtful words with expressions of love and affirmation. Seeking professional guidance and spiritual support can facilitate healing and promote renewed intimacy.

Scripture: **James 1:19**: "My dear brothers and sisters, take note of this: Everyone should be quick to listen, slow to speak and slow to become angry."

Empathy is key. Understanding where our partners are coming from and being there for them is essential, just like **Colossians 3:12-13** teaches us. We've got to create a nurturing environment, especially for our kids.

In conclusion, the words we speak in marriage hold profound implications. Let us strive to use our words wisely, with kindness and love, to nurture and strengthen our spousal relationships. By cultivating mutual respect, empathy, and a commitment to uplifting communication, we can create a marriage grounded in trust, intimacy, and lasting joy.

Verbal poison can corrode spousal relationships, insights into intentional communication and spiritual guidance can foster healing and restoration. Understanding the root causes of verbal abuse and addressing them with compassion and empathy is essential for breaking destructive cycles and fostering a marriage built on love and respect.

A close friend who had been facing significant challenges in her marriage frequently was verbally abused by her husband. This undermined her confidence, causing immense stress, even in front of their three sons. The situation worsened, leading her to consider the difficult decision of leaving her husband to protect herself and her children. The stress became overwhelming, to the point where she was prescribed medication to manage her anxiety.

I emphasised the importance of prayer, seeking spiritual guidance, and leaning on supportive relationships during challenging times. By encouraging her to turn to God and her pastor for strength and wisdom, we're helping her navigate her situation with faith and hope.

Chapter 5

SCARS OF VERBAL ABUSE

Verbal abuse, especially in childhood, can leave deep scars affecting children's psychological well-being as they grow, impacting various aspects of their lives like marriages and workplaces. It's not just about the hurtful words; it's about the long-term effects they can have.

Children are especially vulnerable to the psychological toll of verbal abuse. As they are in their formative years and rely on caregivers for support, they are made more susceptible to internalising negative messages. This can lead to lasting psychological issues that linger into adulthood. Such as:

Fear and Anxiety

Fear and anxiety are common outcomes of verbal abuse in children. Constant exposure to hurtful words can create a sense of dread and hyper-vigilance, causing children to live in a state of fear, always anticipating verbal attacks, even in everyday situations.

Feelings of Inadequacy

A consistent barrage of negative messages can lead to deep-seated feelings of inadequacy and self-loathing. In extreme cases, children may resort to self-harm as a coping mechanism to numb emotional pain and regain a sense of control.

Fear of Rejection

Children subjected to verbal abuse often experience difficulties in forming healthy relationships. The fear of rejection and mistrust stemming from past experiences can lead to social isolation and challenges in establishing meaningful connections with peers and authority figures.

Social Isolation

Social isolation often comes with verbal abuse too. People might withdraw from others to protect themselves from more hurtful words, which just makes them feel even more alone and worthless.

Communication Barriers

The impact of childhood verbal abuse often extends into

adult relationships, particularly within marriages. Adults who experienced verbal mistreatment as children may struggle with trust issues, communication barriers, and emotional intimacy in their relationships.

There was a husband, who found it challenging to express affection towards his wife due to unresolved childhood trauma from verbal abuse. His father's harsh words and demeaning remarks left him emotionally guarded and fearful of vulnerability. As a result, he struggled with trust issues and communication barriers in his marriage, leading to misunderstandings and emotional distance.

Self-harm

Self-harm can be a way for people to deal with the pain from verbal abuse. They might hurt themselves to try and numb the emotional hurt, but it just makes things worse in the long run. This shows how much verbal abuse can mess with someone's head and make them feel really alone.

Eating Disorders

Sometimes, verbal abuse can even lead to eating disorders like anorexia or bulimia. People might start obsessing over their body image or use food to cope with the pain, which only makes things harder for them mentally and physically.

Fear

Fear becomes a prevalent emotion for individuals subjected to verbal abuse in various settings. Fear of judgement, fear of failure, and fear of further mistreatment can dominate their thoughts and actions, hindering their ability to pursue opportunities and engage fully in life.

In the next chapter we will look into how biblical wisdom can help us overcome as we explore the journey of healing and transformation, offering hope and guidance to those who seek solace in the midst of their pain.

Chapter 6

HOW TO RECEIVE HEALING

Healing starts with facing those painful memories head-on and recognising how much they've shaped us. With faith and prayer, we can begin to accept our feelings and take steps toward healing.

Scripture offers wisdom and guidance on healing from the psychological wounds inflicted by verbal abuse. **Psalms 34:17-18 (NIV)** assures us that "The righteous cry out, and the Lord hears them; he delivers them from all their troubles. The Lord is close to the broken hearted and saves those who are crushed in spirit."

Another example of how to be healed from verbal abuse or word curses is in **1 Chronicles 4:9-10:** "Jabez was more honourable than his brothers. His mother had named him Jabez, saying, "I gave birth to him in pain." 10 Jabez cried out to the God of Israel, "Oh, that you would bless me and enlarge my territory! Let your hand be with me, and keep me from harm so that I will be free from pain." And God granted his request.

In this situation, Jabez's name was a curse because whenever he was called, it affirmed he was a child of sorrow. However, he decided to change this through crying to GOD. God can reverse everything spoken over you through prayer.

Understanding the psychological and spiritual effects of verbal abuse is crucial for fostering healing and resilience among individuals affected by this form of mistreatment.

By acknowledging the profound impact of hurtful words on children and adults alike, we can work towards creating supportive environments that promote emotional well-being and restore dignity to those who have suffered from verbal abuse throughout their lives.

In a young woman's journey of practising self-compassion and embracing God's love mirrors the biblical story of the woman at the well (John 4:1-30). Despite facing rejection and judgement from others, Jesus showed her compassion and offered her living water, symbolising spiritual renewal and healing. Similarly, she found solace in God's unwavering love, allowing her to embark on a path of healing and restoration.

In validating their experiences through faith, individuals open themselves to God's comforting presence, trusting that He sees their pain and is ready to guide them towards restoration.

Empowering oneself in the healing journey involves believing in God's unwavering love and healing power. Despite the hurt caused by caregivers, having faith that God understands the depth of the wounds and is ready to lead towards healing is transformative.

Proverbs 3:5-6 (NIV) reminds us, "Trust in the Lord with all your heart and lean not on your own understanding; in all your ways submit to him, and he will make your paths straight." Trusting in God's love and guidance allows individuals to navigate their healing journey with courage and hope.

Healing childhood wounds can be a sprint or a marathon. The more we get a revelation of the word of God and his love, the faster we can be made whole. I know someone who was severely wounded emotionally and carried the wound for over 10 years, but was set free completely by a single sermon. This shows that all we need is a revelation from God's word to be free. Give yourself the time and patience needed to heal from past trauma, stay in God's word and receive the freedom it offers. Understand that the journey towards self-acceptance and healing is unique to each individual and requires perseverance.

Each step towards healing is a testament to God's grace and transformative power. **James 5:11 (NIV)** encourages, "As you know, we count as blessed those who have persevered. You have heard of Job's perseverance and have seen what the Lord finally brought about. The Lord is full of compassion and mercy." Through prayer and patience, individuals can experience God's compassion and mercy in their healing journey.

Remember, God's love is constant and unwavering. He demonstrated His love by sacrificing Himself on the cross for us, and through His wounds, we find healing.

Seeking support from trusted individuals is crucial in the healing process. Avoid isolation and reach out to friends, family, spiritual mentors or counsellors who can provide empathy, guidance, and encouragement. **Proverb 27:17** states, "As iron sharpens iron, so one person sharpens another." It's important that we don't surround ourselves with people who simply nurse our wounds and don't challenge us with loving truth that energises us to put our past behind and embrace our true identity in Christ.

Proverbs 11:14 (NIV) states, "For lack of guidance a nation falls, but victory is won through many advisers." Surround yourself with a supportive community that uplifts and strengthens you on your healing journey.

One evening, I had some friends over, and we had an insightful discussion about the impact of verbal abuse on different areas of life like marriage, education, work, and other relationships. It's a topic I'm deeply passionate about, and my friends know how important it is to me. The bible reminds us to watch what we say.

Ephesians 4:29 (NIV): "Do not let any unwholesome talk come out of your mouths, but only what is helpful for building others up according to their needs, that it may benefit those who listen."

Proverbs 18:21 (NIV): "The tongue has the power of life and death, and those who love it will eat its fruit."

Although verbal abuse can have lasting effects, through resilience, determination, and the Word of God, healing and growth are possible. By fostering environments of kindness and empathy, we can combat the harmful impacts of verbal abuse and promote healing in our communities. So, take some time out to pray and write down your thoughts. Ask God to show you where you need healing and how to move forward.

Talking to someone you trust, like a spiritual mentor or a friend, can also really help. They can give you advice and support based on what the Bible says and help you grow spiritually.

Breaking free from the past means letting go of old habits and ways of thinking that hold you back. It's about finding new, healthier ways to cope and believing in yourself. And don't forget, it's okay to lean on your faith community or friends for support. They can pray for you, listen to you, and help you stay strong on your healing journey. **Hebrews 10:24-25 (NIV)** urges, "And let us consider how we may spur one another on toward love and good deeds, not giving up meeting together, as some are in the habit of doing, but encouraging one another and all the more as you see the Day approaching." Building a supportive community fosters resilience and faith in God's transformative work.

Romans 12:2 (NIV) advises, "Do not conform to the pattern of this world but be transformed by the renewing of your mind. Then you will be able to test and approve what God's will is his good, pleasing and perfect will." By aligning thoughts and behaviours with God's truth through prayer, individuals experience transformation and healing.

Self-care is integral to healing childhood wounds. Prioritising physical, mental, and spiritual well-being through prayer, and nurturing spiritual connections honours God's gift of life and restoration.

Furthermore, another important thing you must do is to use the power of your own words. Start to cancel every negative word that has been spoken or is being spoken against you. Consider **Isaiah 54:17,** "No weapon formed against you shall prosper, And every tongue which rises against you in judgment You shall condemn. This is the heritage of the servants of the Lord, And their righteousness is from Me," Says the Lord. We fulfil this verse by speaking out loud what God says concerning us.

For example, someone says, "You are a useless woman, it will never go well with you." To cancel that you can say, "I reject that in Jesus name! I am blessed on every side and I will see God's goodness in the land of the living."
Say it out loud immediately but in humility to cancel what has been said.

1 Corinthians 6:19-20 (NIV) affirms, "Do you not know that your bodies are temples of the Holy Spirit, who is in you, whom you have received from God? You are not your own; you were bought at a price. Therefore, honour God with your bodies." Practicing self-care aligns with God's desire for holistic healing and restoration.

Seeking counsel and focusing on personal growth, Samantha exemplifies the biblical principle of turning to God for strength and direction. Her journey echoes the stories of resilience found in Scripture, where individuals like Esther and Paul overcame adversity to fulfil their purpose. Through her perseverance, Samantha has transformed her life, inspired hope and reminding us of God's redemptive power in healing the wounds inflicted by verbal abuse.

Breaking the Cycle of Verbal Abuse

Breaking the cycle of verbal abuse requires intentional effort and resilience. Those affected may become passive Survivors, enduring silently and internalising pain, or proactive Victors, determined to break free and cultivate healthy relationships for themselves and future generations.

Breaking the cycle of verbal abuse also requires prayerful healing, a deliberate process of surrendering past wounds and seeking God's transformative work within our hearts and families. Prayer changes things, through prayer, individuals can release emotional burdens, forgive past hurts, and cultivate healthier patterns of communication and behaviour rooted in God's love.

Matthew 11:28 (ESV): "Come to me, all who labour and are heavy laden, and I will give you rest."

Romans 12:2 (ESV): "Do not be conformed to this world, but be transformed by the renewal of your mind, that by testing you may discern what is the will of God, what is good and acceptable and perfect."

Breaking Generational Patterns of Verbal Abuse

This requires faith and prayer. By embracing prayerful and seeking divine intervention in healing and deliverance, individuals can break free from destructive cycles and cultivate a legacy of love, respect, and spiritual transformation for future generations. These patterns may have become demonic strongholds that need to be broken and demons cast out for people to be totally set free.

Let us commit to nurturing a lifestyle of prayer, rooted in faith and guided by God's wisdom, as essential tools for breaking generational patterns of verbal abuse and fostering healing within ourselves and our families. Through prayer, we invite God's grace and transformative power to shape our hearts and relationships, paving the way for a future marked by love, empathy, and spiritual growth.

It's unfortunate that children who experience verbal abuse may miss out on opportunities to become positive role models in society. With the right support and nurturing environment, they could have channelled their potential into meaningful contributions.

The Bible provides guidance on the power of words and the impact they have on individuals. **Proverbs 18:21 (NIV)** states, "The tongue has the power of life and death, and those who love it will eat its fruit." This verse underscores the importance of using words wisely and compassionately, especially in the context of parenting and nurturing children.

Chapter 7

FORGIVENESS

In earlier chapters, we explored how many parents, despite their love for their children, inadvertently engage in verbal abuse due to a lack of awareness and understanding. However, this doesn't excuse their behaviour, as the impact of verbal abuse on children can lead to profound negative repercussions. Children react differently to this treatment; some bear grudges against their parents, while others struggle with forgiveness.

Forgiveness is a vital step in healing from the wounds of verbal abuse. By embracing forgiveness and seeking reconciliation, we can pave the way for healing and restoration in our relationships, guided by the example of God's boundless love and forgiveness.

Verbal abuse can strain the bond between parents and children, leading to negative repercussions that echo through adulthood. Understanding this dynamic is crucial for fostering reconciliation and inner healing.

Forgiveness is a process that can be incredibly challenging, especially when the wounds are deep. Some have struggled with forgiving their caregivers for years of verbal mistreatment. And not until they found solace in the Word of God and understood the power of forgiveness that they were able to mend their relationship.

In the Bible, we see the story of Joseph forgiving his brothers for betraying him and selling him into slavery (Genesis 50:19-21). Despite their wrongdoing, Joseph chose to forgive, recognising that God's plan was at work. This example shows us the transformative power of forgiveness in repairing broken relationships.

Colossians 3:13 (NIV): "Bear with each other and forgive one another if any of you has a grievance against someone. Forgive as the Lord forgave you."

Matthew 6:14-15 (NIV): "For if you forgive other people when they sin against you, your heavenly Father will also forgive you. But if you do not forgive others their sins, your Father will not forgive your sins."

Verbal abuse can create deep wounds that fester over time, leading to bitterness and resentment. However, forgiveness releases us from the emotional bondage of past hurts. Forgiveness is made easier when we remember that we are just as guilty of sin as anyone else before God but he has forgiven us of all our sins.

Ephesians 4:31-32 (NIV): "Get rid of all bitterness, rage and anger, brawling and slander, along with every form of malice. Be kind and compassionate to one another, forgiving each other, just as in Christ God forgave you."

Forgiveness is an act of liberation, freeing us from the weight of resentment and anger.

Colossians 3:13 (NIV): "Bear with each other and forgive one another if any of you has a grievance against someone. Forgive as the Lord forgave you."

Choosing forgiveness leads to personal healing and restores peace within ourselves.

Luke 6:37 (NIV): "Do not judge, and you will not be judged. Do not condemn, and you will not be condemned. Forgive, and you will be forgiven."

Following God's example of forgiveness teaches us to extend grace to others.

Ephesians 4:32 (NIV): "Be kind and compassionate to one another, forgiving each other, just as in Christ God forgave you."

Forgiveness requires wisdom and patience, fostering personal growth and maturity.

Proverbs 19:11 (NIV): "A person's wisdom yields patience; it is to one's glory to overlook an offence."

Chapter 8

REPLACING FEAR WITH FAITH

Verbal abuse can leave lasting scars, but it's crucial to understand that you are not to blame for the hurtful actions of others. Acknowledging this truth is a key step in overcoming fear and self-blame. Remember the story of Moses, who initially struggled with feelings of inadequacy and fear when God called him to lead the Israelites out of Egypt (Exodus 3-4). Despite his doubts, God assured Moses of His presence and empowerment. Like Moses, you are not defined by past hurts or insecurities. God is with you, empowering you to overcome fear and embrace faith.

Be encouraged by the words in **Romans 8:31** which says, "… If God is for us, who can be against us?" God is for you!

He loves you, and His plan for you is good and not evil. Jeremiah 29:11.

Establishing boundaries helps protect your emotional well-being and fosters a sense of safety. Setting a boundary with the promises of God strengthens your faith and weakens the voices of fear. Consider the story of Nehemiah, who demonstrated firm boundaries when leading the rebuilding of Jerusalem's walls (Nehemiah 4). Despite facing opposition and intimidation, Nehemiah remained steadfast in his resolve, relying on God's strength. Like Nehemiah, you can set firm boundaries rooted in faith, guarding your heart and well-being from further harm.

Be kind and compassionate to yourself as you heal from the wounds of verbal abuse. Show yourself the same grace and understanding that God extends to you. Reflect on the story of the prodigal son (Luke 15:11-32), where the father exemplified unconditional love and forgiveness. Just as the father embraced his wayward son with compassion, God extends boundless love and acceptance to you. When we turn to God, we find rest as it's written in **Isaiah 30:15,** "In returning and rest you shall be saved; In quietness and confidence shall be your strength."

Invest in personal spiritual growth and development to overcome limiting beliefs instilled by verbal abuse. Embrace opportunities for learning and self-improvement. Think about the story of Ruth, who exhibited resilience and faithfulness in challenging circumstances (Ruth 1-4). Despite facing loss and hardship, Ruth remained steadfast and embraced God's plan for her life. Like Ruth, focus on personal growth rooted in faith. Spend time in studying the bible, the Word of God to discover the promises of God and His boundless grace and mercy, trusting in His guidance for your journey.

Forgiveness is a powerful tool for healing. Pray for the strength to forgive those who have hurt you, releasing the burden of resentment. Reflect on the story of Jonah, who initially struggled with bitterness towards the people of Nineveh (Jonah 4). Through God's compassion and teaching, Jonah learned the importance of forgiveness and mercy. Allow the Holy Spirit to cultivate a forgiving heart within you, freeing you from the weight of past hurts.

Prayer Points:

Prayer for Emotional Healing:
"Heavenly Father, I come before you seeking healing from the emotional wounds of verbal abuse. Grant me peace and comfort as I navigate through this journey of recovery. Help me to release the burden of fear and replace it with unwavering faith in your love and protection."

Prayer for Forgiveness and Compassion:
"Lord, I surrender my hurt and pain to you. Grant me the grace to forgive those who have spoken words of harm and negativity over my life. Teach me to show compassion towards myself and others, reflecting your boundless mercy. Amen."

By leaning on the support of understanding friends, family, and spiritual mentors, and incorporating prayer and biblical principles into your healing journey, you can overcome fear and cultivate a deep sense of faith and resilience.

Chapter 9

SPOTTING VERBAL ABUSE IN SCHOOLS AND WORKPLACES

In schools and workplaces, verbal abuse can be pervasive, often stemming from bullies who may themselves be replicators of the hurtful words they've heard at home. These bullies target individuals who may be survivors of abuse in their own homes, compounding the cycle of verbal mistreatment. Let's delve into how to identify and address this issue in both educational and professional settings.

In the workplace environments, verbal abuse can affect professional relationships and mental well-being.

Employees who experience verbal mistreatment from colleagues or superiors may struggle with confidence, job satisfaction, and overall productivity.

In schools, it manifests through bullying behaviour, where students target others based on their appearance, intelligence, or perceived weaknesses. These bullies, typically replicating hurtful language and attitudes they've witnessed or experienced, can make victims feel ostracised and unworthy. Consider James, for instance, a bright student who faced relentless teasing for his academic achievements. Such experiences can deeply affect a student's self-esteem and sense of belonging.

The Bible reminds us in **Proverbs 12:18** that "The words of the reckless pierce like swords, but the tongue of the wise brings healing." Verbal abuse in schools can indeed inflict lasting wounds on victims, hindering their academic performance and emotional well-being. It's crucial for educators and administrators to recognise the signs of verbal abuse and create a supportive environment where all students feel safe and valued.

As **Proverbs 18:21** reminds us, "The tongue has the power

of life and death, and those who love it will eat its fruit." Toxic work environments fuelled by verbal abuse can indeed crush the spirit of employees, leading to decreased productivity, increased stress, and compromised mental health. Employers must take proactive steps to foster a culture of respect and kindness, where all employees are treated with dignity and fairness.

Tackling verbal abuse at school and work is key to stopping the cycle of negativity and making everyone feel good about themselves. Let's team up to spread healing and kindness, just like **Ephesians 4:29** says: "Don't say anything that would hurt others. Instead, speak only what is good so that you can give help wherever it's needed. That way, what you say will help those who hear you."

Chapter 10

MOVING FORWARD

In the journey of healing from verbal abuse, finding one's voice and reclaiming personal power are crucial steps towards restoration and growth. This chapter explores strategies for assertiveness and self-empowerment, drawing on the wisdom of scripture, prayer, self-development, and real-life experiences like Julia's.

Strategies for Assertiveness and Self-Empowerment:

"The Lord is my light and my salvation, whom shall I fear? The Lord is the stronghold of my life of whom shall I be afraid?" **(Psalm 27:1)**

Self-compassion is essential in the healing journey, allowing individuals to acknowledge their pain without self-judgment. Julia's experience highlights the importance of understanding and addressing the underlying beliefs shaped by past experiences. By extending grace and understanding to oneself, it becomes possible to cultivate inner peace and resilience.

"Therefore, as God's chosen people, holy and dearly loved, clothe yourselves with compassion, kindness, humility, gentleness and patience." **(Colossians 3:12)**

Setting boundaries is super important for taking care of yourself, and Julia's story really drives that home. It shows how messed up relationships can mess with your ability to trust and connect with others. But when you set boundaries, you're not just protecting yourself, you're saying, "Hey, I deserve respect."

You know that verse from Proverbs, "Guard your heart above all else"? It's like your heart sets the course for your life, so you gotta protect it from all the stuff that can mess it up.

Being assertive is a game-changer. It's about speaking up for yourself in a confident and respectful way. Julia's journey shows how important it is to overcome fear and speak your truth. When you're assertive, you can have healthier relationships and better communication.

And don't forget about **seeking guidance** from mentors or counsellors. They can offer some serious support and insight. Plus, studying the Bible, meditating on what God says concerning you instead of what has been said to you and praying regularly is key for staying grounded and getting through tough times. Julia's story really drives home the importance of leaning on God's Word and strength when life gets tough.

"Trust in the Lord with all your heart and lean not on your own understanding; in all your ways submit to him, and he will make your paths straight." **(Proverbs 3:5-6)**

Chapter 11

MAKING A CHANGE

Your Voice Matters: Advocating for Change and Awareness

In a world where verbal abuse often goes unnoticed or dismissed, it's essential to recognise the power of our voices in advocating for change and raising awareness about this pervasive issue. Each of us has the ability to make a difference, whether it's by speaking up for ourselves, supporting others, or challenging societal norms that tolerate abusive behaviour.

One of the most significant ways we can advocate for change is by empowering victims of verbal abuse to speak out and seek help. By providing resources, support networks, and safe spaces for individuals to share their experiences, we can help them reclaim their voices and take control of their lives.

Just as in the case of a woman who was bullied by her boss. She resolved to take action. She started by speaking up during team meetings, gently reminding her colleagues of the importance of kindness and respect in the workplace. She shared her story with a few trusted coworkers, hoping to shed light on the issue and spark conversations about change.

She reached out to HR, highlighting the prevalence of bullying in the office and advocating for policies to address the issue. She organised workshops on conflict resolution and communication skills, empowering her coworkers to stand up against mistreatment and create a more positive work environment. Despite facing resistance and scepticism from some quarters, She remained steadfast in her mission.

Over time, her efforts began to bear fruit. More and more coworkers started speaking out against bullying, and the office culture slowly began to shift. People felt safer and more supported, and productivity soared as morale improved.

Verbal abuse thrives in environments where it is normalised or overlooked. As advocates, we must challenge the status quo and hold perpetrators accountable for their actions. This may involve advocating for stronger policies and laws against verbal abuse, raising awareness in schools and workplaces, and promoting a culture of respect and empathy.

Many people may not fully understand the impact of their words or realise when they are engaging in verbally abusive behaviour. By educating others about the signs of verbal abuse and the importance of healthy communication, we can create more empathetic and supportive communities where everyone feels valued and respected.

Take a personal responsibility and pay attention to the words you speak to others. We can turn to the wisdom of the Bible for guidance. Ephesians 4:32 reminds us to treat each other with kindness and compassion, setting the tone for healthy relationships.

Your voice holds tremendous significance in the fight against verbal abuse. Through advocating for change, raising awareness, and extending support to victims, we can envision and actively work towards a world where healthy communication and mutual respect prevail. Together, we can shape our community where verbal abuse is replaced with compassion, respect, and love. Just like the Victors of verbal abuse became a force for positive change.

Chapter 12

PRAYER POINTS

These prayer points cover various aspects of healing, strength, guidance, and restoration, drawing from the wisdom and promises found in the scriptures.

Healing

- Heavenly Father, we pray for complete healing from the emotional wounds inflicted by verbal abuse, trusting in Your promise to restore what was broken. (Joel 2:25)

- Lord, help us to find solace in Your presence and comfort in Your embrace as we journey towards healing and wholeness. (Psalm 34:18)

- Father, surround us with Your love and protection, shielding us from the lingering effects of verbal abuse and filling us with Your peace. (Isaiah 41:10)

- Grant us the courage to seek professional help and support on our healing journey, Lord, knowing that You work through the hands of caring professionals. (James 5:16)

- Lord, we thank You for the promise of healing found in Your Word and the assurance that You are with us every step of the way. (Psalm 147:3)

Forgiveness

- Father, help us to release any bitterness or resentment towards those who have hurt us, allowing Your love to flow freely through us. (Ephesians 4:32)

- Lord, grant us the grace to forgive ourselves for any mistakes or shortcomings, knowing that You offer redemption and restoration to all who seek You. (1 John 1:9)

- Help us to let go of the past and embrace the future You have prepared for us, Lord, free from the burden of unforgiveness. (Philippians 3:13-14)

- Heavenly Father, give us the strength to forgive even when it feels impossible, trusting in Your power to heal and transform our hearts. (Matthew 18:21-22)

- Lord, teach us to forgive as You have forgiven us, extending grace and mercy to others as a reflection of Your love. (Colossians 3:13)

Procrastination

- Father, we pray for the discipline and motivation to overcome procrastination and pursue the tasks You have set before us with diligence and purpose. (Proverbs 13:4)

- Lord, help us to prioritise our time and resources wisely, recognising the importance of stewardship in fulfilling Your purposes for our lives. (Ephesians 5:15-16)

- Grant us the courage to step out in faith and take

action, trusting in Your guidance and provision every step of the way. (James 2:17)

- Heavenly Father, break the chains of procrastination that hold us back from fulfilling our potential and walking in the abundance You have promised. (Philippians 4:13)

- Lord, ignite a passion within us to pursue excellence in all that we do, knowing that we do not labor in vain when we work unto You. (1 Corinthians 15:58)

Faith over Fear

- Lord, strengthen our faith and grant us the courage to face our fears with confidence, knowing that You are with us always. (Isaiah 41:10)

- Heavenly Father, replace our fears and doubts with faith and trust in Your unfailing love and faithfulness. (Psalm 56:3)

- Grant us boldness and perseverance in the face of adversity, Lord, as we place our trust in Your promises and provision. (2 Timothy 1:7)

- Lord, help us to stand firm on Your Word and resist the spirit of fear, knowing that You have given us a spirit of power, love, and a sound mind. (Joshua 1:9)

- Heavenly Father, banish all fear and anxiety from our hearts, filling us instead with Your peace that surpasses all understanding. (Philippians 4:6-7)

Overcoming Limitations

- Father, we surrender our limitations and weaknesses to You, trusting in Your strength and sufficiency to carry us through every challenge. (2 Corinthians 12:9)

- Lord, break down the barriers of self-doubt and insecurity that hinder us from stepping into the fullness of Your purpose for our lives. (Philippians 4:13)

- Grant us the wisdom to recognise and overcome the limitations we place on ourselves, Lord, as we surrender to Your plans and purposes. (Jeremiah 29:11)

- Heavenly Father, empower us to break free from the chains of our past and embrace the limitless possibilities that await us in You. (Isaiah 43:18-19)

- Lord, help us to walk in confidence and boldness, knowing that You have equipped us with everything we need to fulfil Your calling on our lives. (Ephesians 3:20)

God's Love and Protection

- Father, thank You for Your unending love and protection, surrounding us with Your presence and guarding us from harm. (Psalm 91:11)

- Lord, help us to trust in Your faithfulness and take refuge in the shelter of Your wings, knowing that You are our fortress and stronghold. (Psalm 18:2)

- Grant us peace and assurance in the knowledge that Your love never fails, and Your mercy endures forever. (Psalm 136:26)
- Heavenly Father, guide us in the paths of righteousness and lead us beside still waters,

refreshing our souls with Your presence. (Psalm 23:3-4)

- Lord, we rest in Your promise to never leave us nor forsake us, finding comfort and strength in Your unfailing love. (Deuteronomy 31:6)

Peace

- Father, we pray for Your peace that surpasses all understanding to guard our hearts and minds in Christ Jesus, anchoring us in the midst of life's storms. (Philippians 4:7)

- Lord, grant us inner peace and tranquility, even in the face of uncertainty and turmoil, knowing that You are in control of all things. (John 14:27)

- Heavenly Father, fill us with Your peace that calms our fears and soothes our anxieties, restoring harmony and wholeness to our souls. (Isaiah 26:3)

- Grant us the grace to let go of worry and anxiety, Lord, as we place our trust in Your unfailing love and providence. (Matthew 6:25-26)

- Lord, may Your peace reign in our relationships and interactions, fostering unity and understanding among us as we walk in Your love. (Colossians 3:15)

Strength and Resilience

- Father, strengthen us with Your mighty power and equip us with endurance and perseverance to overcome every obstacle that stands in our way. (Ephesians 6:10)

- Lord, grant us resilience in the face of adversity, enabling us to rise above challenges and emerge stronger and wiser than before. (Romans 5:3-5)

- Heavenly Father, fill us with courage and boldness to face each day with confidence, knowing that You go before us and fight our battles on our behalf. (Deuteronomy 31:6)

- Grant us the strength to press on towards the goal, Lord, with unwavering faith and determination, trusting in Your promises to sustain us. (Philippians 3:13-14)

- Lord, may we find our strength and refuge in You alone, knowing that You are our rock and fortress, our deliverer in whom we trust. (Psalm 18:2)

Renewed Mindset

- Father, renew our minds and transform our thoughts, replacing negativity and doubt with Your truth and promises of hope and redemption. (Romans 12:2)

- Lord, help us to see ourselves as You see us, fearfully and wonderfully made, with a purpose and destiny ordained by Your love. (Psalm 139:14)

- Heavenly Father, free us from the grip of limiting beliefs and self-doubt, empowering us to step into the fullness of who You created us to be. (2 Corinthians 10:5)

- Grant us clarity of mind and discernment, Lord, to recognise and reject the lies of the enemy, standing firm in the truth of Your Word. (Ephesians 6:14)

- Lord, fill us with Your wisdom and understanding, guiding our thoughts and actions according to Your perfect will and purpose for our lives. (James 1:5)

Gratitude and Contentment

- Father, cultivate within us a spirit of gratitude and contentment, helping us to find joy and fulfilment in the blessings that surround us each day. (1 Thessalonians 5:18)

- Lord, open our eyes to see the beauty and goodness in every situation, even amidst trials and challenges, knowing that You work all things together for our good. (Romans 8:28)

- Heavenly Father, teach us to appreciate the simple pleasures of life and to find satisfaction in Your presence, for in You alone do we find true fulfilment. (Psalm 16:11)

- Grant us the grace to live with open hearts and hands, Lord, sharing generously with others and spreading Your love and kindness wherever we go.

(2 Corinthians 9:7)

- Lord, help us to cultivate a heart of contentment that is rooted in You, trusting in Your provision and sovereignty over every aspect of our lives. (Philippians 4:11-12)

Strength and Resilience

- Father, strengthen us with Your mighty power in our inner being, equipping us to face challenges with courage and perseverance. (Ephesians 3:16)

- Lord, grant us resilience in the face of adversity, enabling us to rise above trials and tribulations with unwavering faith in Your promises. (James 1:12)

- Heavenly Father, fortify our spirits with Your peace that surpasses understanding, anchoring us amidst life's storms and uncertainties. (Philippians 4:7)

- Grant us boldness and determination, Lord, to pursue Your purpose for our lives with unwavering resolve and steadfast faith. (Joshua 1:9)

- Lord, empower us to be overcomers, triumphing over every obstacle and adversity through the victory we have in Christ. (1 John 5:4)

Empowerment and Purpose

- Father, ignite within us a passion for Your kingdom and a desire to make a difference in the world around us, using our gifts and talents for Your glory. (1 Peter 4:10)

- Lord, reveal to us the unique purpose and calling You have placed upon our lives, guiding us into alignment with Your divine plan and destiny. (Jeremiah 29:11)

- Heavenly Father, grant us the wisdom and discernment to recognise opportunities for growth and transformation, seizing each moment as a chance to glorify You. (Colossians 3:23)

- Fill us with Your Spirit, Lord, empowering us to walk in obedience and fulfil the good works You have prepared for us in advance. (Ephesians 2:10)

Prayer Points

- Lord, may Your light shine brightly through us, illuminating the darkness and drawing others into the abundant life found in You. (Matthew 5:16)

OTHER BOOK BY THE AUTHOR

Coming Soon

Sunrise & Sunset Devotional

An easy to use morning and evening devotional journal designed to guide you through a transformative journey in your christian walk, covering various topics over 15-day intervals.

antoniaagbonkpolor.com

www.ingramcontent.com/pod-product-compliance
Lightning Source LLC
Chambersburg PA
CBHW070310120526
44590CB00017B/2621